From These Roots Up

poems by

Kiana Davis

Tree Root Strong Publishings, LLC

From These Roots Up

I am the daughter
of the brokenhearted
sent to breathe again
and set all past fears on fire
and to extinguish
the hollowness of regrets
all roads they were too afraid to travel
I will climb.

I dedicate this book to my Mother, Collinda, Kevin, Wanda and Richard Stewart, Mrs. Betty Calfee and to all those who've reached back to save those left behind.

This project was supported, in part, by an award from 4Culture

Table of Contents

CHAPTER 1
ENTRENCHED

CHAPTER 2
ROOTS AT MY FEET

CHAPTER 3
MISSING LIMBS

CHAPTER 4
TRUNK WITHIN MY TREE

CHAPTER 5
TREE ROOT STRONG

Chapter 1

Entrenched

We are greater than where we've been planted.

Projects

I grew up
below the lines of poverty
raised in America's public housing
I watched as many devised
 plans for survival and escape.

I ate from their table
government cheese and powdered milk,
attended their failing schools,
in a single-parent home
statistics said I would be:
a dropout,
a teenage mother,
a welfare queen,
habitually depending on government assistance,
uneducated,
a black woman too hard for love,
and trapped in a spiral of pain
show her no humanity.

But God
gave me three eyes,
a solace in books,
a love for words,
and an "I Have A Dream" Foundation scholarship.

I continued
so I could extend my hands
to share my story
to give as it was given to me
others extended their hands to me
so I implore you to be saved.

Where I Lived

Solutions to pursue truth
have been drowned out
by the all-consuming flames of:
hunger, underemployment, limited resources,
filth, smells, violence, inadequate schools,
frustration, anger, hopelessness, food deserts,
and the manufactured war on drugs
drugs pumped into poor communities
to annihilate families, cultures,
and a sense of community.

We've cried foul and are told
that our pain is a figment of our imaginations
yet institutional practices, laws and systems
have been built
the aftermath of our emancipation.

To reclaim the streets
we were given the task
of saving ourselves
offered heavy police presence,
a carnage of our sons,
and black and brown bodies
poured into overcrowded
jails and prisons
reminiscent of slave ships.

Unaccounted for

I remember the brokenness
the trash, isolation, and fear
we were unaccounted for
left after the movement,
infiltration of drugs,
murdered and silenced leadership
we were left to forge bonds
with the very streets
we were terrified of
fused worlds to create a culture
to survive.

our words,
our way of life,
our style,
our bravado,
even how we loved,
how we gave,
and how we took
had to yield to brashness of the streets.

picked and pulled apart by systems
as if hoping for our self-destruction.
but the frayed pieces of our DNA
kept us from death.

Back Then

Back then
a little girl black with pressed hair
wrapping towels around my head
believing in beauty one sided
I wanted my daddy home with me
like Mr. Brady.

Back then
searching shelves for
black Ken dolls
until I was twelve
and then I gave all my dolls
to my baby sister,
but she was indifferent to make-believe.

Back then
I just wanted to live
in the privileged TV/book
paradigm where they lived,
always attesting to perfection-
so mama didn't have to work
and have to raise seven children alone.

Back then
I wanted the American dream
for my brothers
so they didn't have
to hang out on corners
being cool for a living.

Back then……..

Drowning

To uphold street honor
two of my brothers
have drowned
beneath the rubble
of lost time
serving unredeemable
portions of their lives
behind bars
in their absence
we've carried shame
blaming them, not for their guilt
but for becoming
victims of the land mines
lying await for brown skin.

Maslow's Hierarchy

To walk among the dead
sanity is often maintained
with claws
escape is a river
and religion,
drugs, alcohol,
sex, and denial are rafts
offering the temporary
gift of escape
and hope
is a distant shore
a journey
everyone is unable to travel.

Rage

Bitterness forces
anger to rise
and composure
is judged by those
who have never lived
with the thin line
between daily traumas
and systematic oppression.

Black History Month

28 days out of a year
crammed accomplishments
out of thin air
and then absence
intentional omissions
and for the remaining 337 days
we were forced
to internalize the disregard
sitting in classrooms bored
no place in America's
text books or dreams
our parents passed
down the little they'd learned
but our future aspirations mirrored
media's beliefs about black and brown worth
with limited names
of leaders on our tongues
and no sense of community
we were disillusioned.

School

They questioned
our brilliance
to ease learned fears
we memorized stories
that gave our voices
no sound
no real anchor
we were
invisible participants
inside our own education.

Names

We were given names
to recapture the sounds
of languages taken from us
some were pulled from books
building roots
to an unknown homeland
and others were sculpted
creating sounds that resembled
all that was lost to us
we were children carrying names
that gave birth to a need
to bridge us closer to a loss
too great to touch.

War Games

To suppress the victimization
wars have been waged
brother against brother
communities have been decimated,
children have been lost,
manufactured genocide has been sold,
families have been torn apart ,
and a steady looping stream of images
criminalizing black and brown skin
has been a daily source of programing.

Drum

This beat
you covet
and pass on as your own
is a living drum
that beats
our Hearts.

We were born
from storytellers
born to retell
our life stories
placing traumas
inside melodies
our art therapy:
dancing,
singing
to live another day
Unbroken.

Chapter 2

Roots at my Feet

*For my mother and the women in our family
and community, who were afraid
I would tread their roads.*

Keep on Living

Independent life warriors
our mother pushed
her daughters
out of the nest
teaching us to fly
without fully formed wings
afraid of hitting the ground
our cries seemed to question
her maternal instincts:
"Are you hurt?
come here- let me look at you.
Girl, you all right there is nothing
wrong with you-get up and keep on living."

Chasing Rainbows

My mother's eyes
shine with optimism
and she says:
"maybe he will change in there."

but my hope
for his reform is jaded:
"he will change
when he wakes up
and is ready to listen."

as if I have spoken
in another language
she stares through me
and I realized
she would always chase
rainbows for her sons.

Spirituals

I never understood
the weight of her songs
or the way she sang them
Sunday mornings cooking breakfast

She stopped often
to hang her head
before the sink-
the song stretched
throughout our home,
a hovering presence
we could not name

Her voice
pulled the song
high above our heads
No one spoke
when she was like this
we just listened
and stared at each other
waiting for the angels
to fall like rain
from the ceiling.

Warrior

She
is my mother warrior
who taught me
through her silence
the power of words

she raised us alone
in poverty's bowels
working tirelessly
to provide for us

bore scars
from our fathers blows
so I would never endure
love on battlefields

she encouraged me
to follow my dreams
and go places
she has never known
so I could be free.

The Weight

Oscillating scales
put our weight
at a disadvantage
when she chose him
he punished us
he punished her
when she chose us.

Lessons

Before our eyes
she endured
beatings
and name-calling
to be loved
by our fathers,
whose rage
left us all
hiding scars

Inadvertently,
her life lessons
taught me
to stand tall
within myself
and to only
draw water
from hands
that never tried
to bleed me dry.

Poetic Therapy

Poetry saved me
and my mother
haunted the pages of my journals
to know me
but I learned to script
cryptic messages
twisting my truth
and veiling my secrets
from her invasions.

Fruition

They would come over,
women supposed to be
family and friends
and change the color
of my mother's eyes
speaking small curses
over her children.

I was six or seven
and I watched them
one day watch me:
with glassy eyes
and mocking disdain.

I dared myself
to stare back at them
without blinking-
and they all agreed
that my defiance
came from bad blood
and ways from a father
I never knew.

These Women,
who could not envision
a better life for me
because I was my mother's child,
the fourth of her seven blessings
we were held over her head.

And they spoke hardships
over my life
but God blessed
me with three eyes
a spirit to gather voices-
so roots
never grew from their words
to tie down my feet.

Whole

I didn't want to be the girl
they referred to-
the one they said
they found behind my eye
examining me,
a young girl,
they tried to count
the babies in my future.

But I remained Whole

Suspicious women
who loved too soon
and had babies
too young.

Women who, too
were raised under
watchful eyes,
but cracked
at their beliefs in love.

But I remained Whole
Growing up with

double standards
Mama's baby
Daddy's maybe.

I remained Whole.

Church Mothers

Fanning air
heavy handed women
invoked spirits.

Moving their tired bodies
to the incessant beat
of tambourines and drums
fused with moans of praise
and loud speaking tongues.

I sat back and watched
sitting still
afraid that my movement
would draw sharp eyes
because God was moving.

In Holy Ghost trances-
they danced and sang
knowing their pain was not in vain
and they were being heard.

I watched as the spirit passed them
one by one
shaking them until they fell to the floor
and ushers would
race to cover them with white sheets.

Some waited lifetimes for change
resting by Faith
trying to hold onto their praise
during storms.

Heavy handed
Church Mothers
shaped my belief in miracles
and taught me
that I could tear down
mountains with my mind.

Chapter 3

Missing Limbs

You scattered your seed
without waiting to see
what would bloom
without having father's arms.

On My Tongue

There are no other words
on my tongue
no memory of you that conjures
a connection or feeling
tied by blood,
as if I share
the genealogy of a ghost

There are no other words
on my tongue
but your first name.

Biological

Rough hands
gave me away
before I was able to learn
who I was apart from myself.

Even now
I stare into the faces of strangers
trying to find my features in men
old enough to be him
searching for something in their eyes
that mirror my reflection and reveal my past.

And learning to believe
it wasn't my fault that he left me
barely 18 months old
and ask him how he felt
when he held me knowing he would
never see me grow up
knowing that I'd forget his face-
and he'd lose mine.

I think of him
whenever I see men
holding their babies in safety
kissing their anxieties away.

Idle Corners

I used to see
grown men
stand all day
on idle corners
sipping their libations
and cradling brown paper bags
like they were newborn babies,
fragile extensions of themselves.

I never knew what ailed them
I used to frown and sometimes
I'd laugh at their clumsy drunkenness
but I remember wishing
one of them was strong enough
to be my father.

Woman Strong

Back then
I didn't understand that
my daddy/father/biological
who I have never laid
eyes upon since my heart
could hold memories
was simply a man,
struggling with sobriety
and who could not
love himself enough
to raise me into woman.

The Half Daughter

My father's whole daughter
found me,
24 years later:
unearthing
suppressed questions
about my other half.

I learned that
she had known of me
ever since
she was a little girl
because our father
had once carried
my worn baby picture
in his wallet.

I admitted
I envied the fact
that she had a father
to raise her whole-
but she told me
I was the lucky one.

Revenge

I blamed you
silently for years
for not being there
for me
and built my own
personal monuments of happiness
so that wherever you looked
you could not avoid me
and you would have to carry me
haunted by the ghosts
of your loss.

Steady Father Figure

The only steady father figure
I knew as a child
was my older brother,
Michael
who was too young
for the weight-
and couldn't raise us
passed first steps
or first words.

Surrogate Love

We are daughters
that have to ask strangers
to walk us down the aisle
young girls to women
who God has blessed
with father figures
who will hold our arms-
and give us surrogate love.

Chapter 4

Trunk within my Tree

Dedicated to my older brother Kevin:
You will always be with me
the trunk within my tree.

Kevin's Rainbow

We walked through
rainbows together
through colored beads
hanging from the ceiling
in the hallway.

We pulled them down
secretly making jewelry for me
and whips for you.

Three years older
you held my hand
when we crossed the street
marveling at diesel trucks
you vowed
that you would one day
ride the backs of their doors
and survive the impact.

I was five
when you attempted
the stunt without me
and days later

we sat in darkness
as a Minister
recited a eulogy for you.

I wondered
why it was so dark
and why everyone
shook with trembles sobbing.
I twirled black beads
around my hands
a woman in tears
had given me.
and I remembered
our rainbow
and waited for you
to climb out of the dirt
and hand me the roses
being tossed
onto your casket.

Where I Could not Follow

I knew
my brother's idea
for all of us
to look through
old photo albums
was a way
for him to say goodbye to us.

That night
we huddled together
on our mother's bed
laughing with our backs
pressed against the headboard
laughing at our favorite memories.

I knew
when he would not
hold my smile
with his eyes
but looked away from me-
that he was going
where I could not follow.

After Kevin

After you left
they came by twos
heavy women,
with their own
crosses to bear
and filled our home
with mourning.

I slipped through
the cracks
their bodies made
and stood
in the center
of my mother's storm
spinning
then falling
whispering
Ring Around a Rosie
thinking it was all a game.

I wanted to tell them
you came to me
in a dream
and we spoke
standing by the train tracks

and that you told me
you couldn't come home-
but you were safe
on the other side
and no,
I could not
cross the tracks
to be with you.

But they chanted
pulling me away
from the circle
crying for answers exhausted.

Grief

After the loss of Kevin
my mother broke down
and began seeking answers

At seven
she taught me
how to meditate
I remember
lying next to her
eyes closed

Repeatedly we chanted:
Om, Om, Om
until it became
a hushed whisper between us
and my body soared
on a flight of weightlessness.

Kevin's Summer

There is no place to call home
all the walls that once contained
first memories
have been dismantled
every poem
makes me travel in time
and together
we live
eternal summer days
whenever I am near a pen
you exist again.

Chapter 5

Tree Root Strong

I stood on the roots of trees as a child
believing they would make me stronger
than the madness around me.

From These Roots up

I caught tadpoles
in a creek at the dead end of my block
holding my childhood
under punctured jelly jar lids.
climbed linked silver fences
to play in fields overgrown
to capture butterflies.

catching butterflies
was my bridge
to another life.

I ate blackberries year-round
and rode my bike through
the safest places I could find
not wanting the tea parties to end
or to lose track of my imaginary friends.

One Summer

I hung a swing from my favorite tree
by a thin rope tied to a black tire
when I did not fall-
a small crowd formed around me
and I watched their eyes-
they were so eager to be grown
always dismissing me
because I never tried to push time beyond its limits.
Their eyes followed my movement
and I could read their contempt
but they all stayed
standing on my roots
for their turn.

Memories

Dedicated to my older sister Collinda

To stop our world from crumbling
you held out your hands
and carried everything you could
to help keep us above the madness
but terror and instability
can make anyone
despise forms of vulnerability
and innocent encounters
can cause a reliving of the past
and you must travel back
to a time
when you were too young
to navigate the world alone
and the hands that promised
to protect you
could not always be trusted.

Twisted

We shared a part
of the same twisted path-
where the cycle of motherhood
often began as early as sixteen.

We've both watched
scenes of anger, shame, and self-doubt
explode into violence
watching men stand on corners idle
drinking truth at bay.

We've witnessed dark fists
beat our mothers, our sisters,
and even our own bodies
have scars from blows
meant to reinforce manhood.

A few years older than me
I watched you live with a man
in a cruel place you called love
We were entrenched on similar roads
but I chose the one less traveled by.

Beyond the Walls

Dedicated to Mom Stewart

She spoke of life beyond the walls
and gave me the dream of college
she had the power
to tell it like it was
and I listened
because her words
were first given
to me in visions
and they beat
through me truth.

My Something Good

In the third grade
I knew something good
was coming to me- and if I held on
like the knowing told me
I would reap my good.

Each year I waited
questioning the silent peace-
and still small voices
but I remembered Kevin
and the knowing before he died.

In the sixth grade my principal
told us that our class
was being sponsored
by the "I Have A Dream" Foundation-
and he spoke of college.

Instantly I knew
my way out had been paved
and I stared back at him
smiling inside
his smile grew
as he tried to get me to see
what the opportunity meant-but I could only nod
and stare through him into my knowing.

Vision

Where there is no vision, the people perish... Proverb 29:18

I lived it
twelve years
where light shined
but never really
touched the eyes of its people
there were few visions
beyond the corners
and for many
getting out was mocked
who wanted to get out?
hell was too comfortable a place.
I knew I'd be saved
as a young child-
I could easily
see over enough
to jump out.

Storyteller

Inspired by poet Yusef Komunyakaa

He makes me think of dirt roads
southern Black ways
building a culture from the scraps
and fringes of memories
fusing two worlds into mine
his words take me to hot churches,
heavy handed neighbors, and
cobblers filled with handpicked blackberries
he carries my brother in his stories
who died believing in white magic
he has become my gateway
retelling the past with cloudy eyes for me.

Touch

I can recall the ugliness
I don't need to bend memories
to recount the imperfections
that don't fit the standards
we are conditioned to reach for
but there was beauty
and so much strength
among the chaos.

If I could touch the spirit
of my childhood bliss,
I would be reborn.

About the Author:

Kiana Davis was born and raised in North Richmond, California. She began writing poetry at the age of 12 to grapple with growing up in poverty.

For over 10 years, she has worked as an educator teaching at-risk youth in Washington State.

In 2014 Kiana was awarded a 4Culture Individual Heritage grant. The grant will allow her to publish her second collection of poetry, and gift copies to under-served youth living in South King County.